WW kitchen collection

One pot

Simple, tasty family favourite
Quorn sausage pasta bake, page 24

Winter warmer full of flavour
Smoked paprika beef goulash, page 90

Traditional and hearty bake
Potato, onion & bacon hotpot, page 80

Sweet & sour, Chinese-style
Quick pineapple & pork stir-fry, page 92

WW kitchen collection

One pot

The small print

EGGS We use medium eggs, unless otherwise stated. Pregnant women, the elderly and children should avoid recipes with eggs which are not fully cooked or raw.

FRUIT AND VEGETABLES Recipes use medium-sized fruit and veg, unless otherwise stated.

REDUCED FAT SOFT CHEESE Where a recipe uses reduced fat soft cheese, we mean a soft cheese with 30% less fat than its full fat equivalent.

LOW FAT SPREAD When a recipe uses a low fat spread, we mean a spread with a fat content of no more than 39%

MICROWAVES If we have used a microwave in any of our recipes, the timings will be for an 850 watt microwave oven.

PREP AND COOKING TIMES These are approximate and meant to be guidelines. Prep time includes all the steps up to and following the main cooking time(s). Cooking times may vary according to your oven.

GLUTEN FREE The use of the term 'gluten free' or the 'gluten free icon' is illustrative only. Weight Watchers is not responsible for the presence of gluten in the dishes that have not been prepared in accordance with instructions; nor is it responsible for gluten contamination due to an external cause. Recipes labelled as gluten free, or displaying the gluten free icon, only include ingredients that naturally do not contain gluten. Whenever using canned, bottled or other types of packaged processed ingredients, such as sauces and stocks, it is essential to check that those ingredients do not contain gluten.

SmartPoints have been calculated using the values for generic foods, not brands (except where stated). Tracking using branded items may affect the recorded SmartPoints.

Seven.

Produced by Seven Publishing on behalf of Weight Watchers International, Inc. Published November 2016. All rights reserved. No part of this publication may be reproduced, stored in a retrieval system or transmitted in any form by any means, electronic, mechanical photocopying, recording or otherwise, without the prior written permission of Seven Publishing.

First published in Great Britain by Seven Publishing Ltd. Copyright © 2016, Weight Watchers International, Inc.

Seven Publishing Ltd
3-7 Herbal Hill
London
EC1R 5EJ
www.seven.co.uk

This book is copyright under the Berne Convention. No reproduction without permission. All rights reserved.

10 9 8 7 6 5 4 3 2 1

Weight Watchers SmartPoints and the SmartPoints icon are the registered trademarks of Weight Watchers International, Inc and are used under license by Weight Watchers (UK) Ltd. All rights reserved.

A CIP catalogue record for this book is available from the British Library. ISBN: 978-0-9935835-3-7

WEIGHT WATCHERS PUBLICATIONS TEAM Imogen Prescott, Samantha Rees, Nicola Kirk, Stephanie Williams, Danielle Smith

PHOTOGRAPHY Alex Luck, Steve Baxter, Jonathan Kennedy, Kris Kirkham, Lauren Mclean, Ria Osborne, William Shaw, Andrew Shaylor, Sam Stowell

RECIPES & FOOD STYLING Sarah Cook, Sarah Akhurst, Sue Ashworth, Kate Blinman, Linzi Brechin, Nadine Brown, Sara Buenfeld, Tamsin Burnett-Hall, Angela Drake, Gabriella English, Marisa Viola Fullarton, Nicola Graimes, Catherine Hill, Laura Kettle, Jenna Leiter, Bianca Nice, Mima Sinclair, Vicki Smallwood, Penny Stephens, Carol Tennant, Polly Webb-Wilson, Hannah Yeadon

PROP STYLING Luis Peral, Linda Berlin, Sarah Birks, Tamzin Ferdinando, Liz Hippisley, Jenny Iggleden, Zoe Regoczy, Carol Tennant, Olivia Wardle

FOR SEVEN PUBLISHING LTD

EDITORIAL & DESIGN
Editor-in-Chief Helen Renshaw **Editor** Ward Hellewell
Art director Liz Baird **Picture editor** Carl Palmer

ACCOUNT MANAGEMENT
Account manager Jo Brennan **Business director, retail** Andy Roughton, **Group publishing director** Kirsten Price

PRODUCTION
Production director Sophie Dillon
Colour reproduction by F1 Colour **Printed in Italy** by L.E.G.O S.p.A

Contents

What could be simpler than

a tasty home-cooked meal that's cooked in a single pot or pan? For one thing, there's **less washing up** afterwards, but one-pot cooking has lots of other benefits, too.

It makes for much simpler recipes since all the elements of the meal are cooked together, and with most one-pot dishes you can serve the meal in the same dish it's cooked in. Many one-pot recipes also lend themselves to **batch cooking and freezing**, saving you even more time in the kitchen later on.

This book brings together some of the most popular **all-in-one recipes** from the Weight Watchers kitchen. From slow-cooked stews, to quick-as-a-flash stir fries, comforting risottos and hearty soups, these recipes are as varied as they are versatile.

Each one has been **tried and tested**, and we've worked out all the SmartPoints, making it easy for you to fit them into your eating plan.

LOOK OUT FOR THE SYMBOLS BELOW:

 The number inside the SmartPoints coin tells you how many SmartPoints are in the serving.

If you're following No Count, you can eat this recipe to your satisfaction without having to count it.

GF A recipe that is totally gluten free, or can be made gluten free with a few simple swaps. Always check labels, as some ingredients, such as baking powder, may contain gluten.

V Indicates a recipe that is vegetarian.

for one-pot cooking

With just a little bit of know-how and a few tips and tricks, you'll find one pot cooking simple and straightforward…

Stock up
There are some ingredients you'll use again and again in one pot cooking, so stock up your store cupboard with tinned tomatoes and other vegetables such as sweetcorn, tinned pulses and beans, barley, risotto and paella rice, dried herbs, spices, stock cubes, coconut milk, soy sauce and Thai fish sauce.

The right equipment
One pot cooking doesn't require lots of equipment – a lidded ovenproof casserole dish, a deep frying pan or wok (also with a lid), a large heavy-based saucepan and a roasting tin are all you will need to make all of the recipes in this book.

Batch cooking
Many one pot recipes lend themselves to batch cooking. For most soups, stews and casseroles, recipe quantities can be doubled, so take advantage of cheaper, seasonal produce to cook larger quantities and freeze them for later.

It's all in the preparation
Part of the secret to successful one pot cooking is in the preparation – in fact, with many one pot dishes, once the initial work is done, you can just leave them to cook and get on with something else. A useful tip is to cut ingredients into similar size pieces to ensure even cooking.

Boost the flavours
One pot recipes benefit from plenty of robust flavour, which will develop over time – many dishes will taste better the next day. Don't be afraid to use ingredients like herbs and spices, lemon zest, balsamic vinegar and tomato purée to give your recipes a real boost.

Go for a garnish
Add another burst of fresh flavour at the end of the cooking time with garnishes such as fresh herbs, a dollop of yogurt or a wedge of lemon.

On the side
Most one pot dishes are complete meals in themselves, but if you do want to serve extras on the side, try a garden salad, a crusty bread roll or brown rice. Don't forget to add any extra SmartPoints.

From oven to table
One of the big benefits of one pot cooking is that there's less washing up to do. Keep it to an absolute minimum by serving the food in the dish you cooked it in.

Make it snappy
While some one pot dishes benefit from lengthy cooking time, others are perfect when you're in a hurry. Stir-fries are cooked in just minutes, and if you're really pressed for time, use ready-prepped veg from the supermarket.

Fancy a side?
Try these (serving sizes shown are per person):
150g boiled new potatoes – 3 extra SmartPoints.
150g cooked brown rice – 6 extra SmartPoints.
150g cooked white rice – 6 extra SmartPoints.
150g prepared cousous – 6 extra SmartPoints.

One pot specials

From slow-cooked wintery casseroles to quick and colourful stir-fries, one pot cooking embraces a wide variety of delicious dishes, suitable for every season.

Casseroles

When the colder weather starts to bite, a classic casserole is hard to beat. They're cooked in the oven in a covered dish, so once you've done all the preparation, your work is over – you barely even have to stir! Casseroles are ideal for inexpensive cuts of meat – the slow cooking in the oven gives a meltingly tender result. Try: Simple beef casserole, p86; Smoked paprika beef goulash, p90.

Stir-fries

Great for quick, fresh tasting meals in warmer weather, stir-fries can be cooked in either a wok or a heavy-based nonstick frying pan. Use plenty of fresh veg with smaller amounts of lean meat. Avoid ready-made sauces with lots of sugar and use Asian-style sauces such as soy or fish sauce and fresh garlic, ginger and chilli instead. Try Turkey stir-fry, p58; Pineapple & pork stir-fry, p92.

Risottos

The classic Italian one pot dish in which rice is cooked in stock to creamy perfection. Butter, cream or cheese are usually added, but there are lots of healthier variations, such as Beetroot and pea risotto, p26. The only downside is that you have to constantly stir most risottos, but if you can't be doing with that, try the Spanish version – paella, p70. You just cover it with a lid and return when cooked.

Soups

There aren't many dishes that are as easy and as varied as soup. With a whole world of different types to choose from, soups can be made cheaply and quickly, and they're great for using up odds and ends in the fridge. Keep them light and fresh, in warmer months, or make them heartier by adding barley, rice or pasta shapes. Try: Spicy prawn laksa, p74; Borlotti bean soup with pancetta, p96; Caldo verde, p100.

Bakes

A great family-friendly option that couldn't be simpler – arrange your meat and veg in a roasting dish, put it in the oven and leave it until it's cooked. You can use just about any ingredient you like, but chicken pieces are a great choice to start with and vegetables like sweet potatoes, carrots, and peppers all work well. Add interest with dried or fresh herbs and spices. Try: Fennel roasted peppers, p16; All-in-one roast chicken, p48.

Stews

Stews can be pretty much anything that's cooked in stock or other liquid in one pot on a stove top. A heavy-based, lidded saucepan is all you will need. Like casseroles, many stews can benefit from slower cooking, but others are quicker to make. Think fragrant curries, spicy chilli con carne, and creamy stroganoff, as well as traditional favourites like classic seafood stew, p68; Spring lamb stew, p78.

Veggie

Try this

Leave out the chilli if you don't like things too spicy. You could use fresh coriander or basil instead of the parsley.

Serves 4

Prep time
15 minutes

Cook time
30 minutes

Ingredients
Calorie controlled cooking spray
1 onion, finely diced
½ teaspoon each fennel and cumin seeds
2 garlic cloves, crushed
1 red chilli, deseeded and finely chopped
1 teaspoon smoked paprika
¼ teaspoon cayenne pepper
1 red and 1 yellow pepper, deseeded and finely sliced
Grated zest of ½ lemon
2 x 400g tins chopped tomatoes
400g tin black beans, drained and rinsed
75g baby leaf spinach
4 eggs
30g feta, crumbled
3 tablespoons chopped fresh flat-leaf parsley

VEGGIE

Black bean shakshuka

Great for breakfast, lunch or dinner, this versatile Middle Eastern dish is bursting with flavour.

1 Mist a medium frying pan with cooking spray. Fry the onion with the fennel seeds and cumin seeds over a medium heat until the onion is soft – about 10 minutes. Add a splash of water if it starts to get too dry.

2 Add the garlic and chilli, and cook for 2-3 minutes. Toss in the ground spices and peppers, frying until the peppers are just soft. Stir in the zest and tomatoes; simmer for 5 minutes.

3 Add the beans and spinach, and season to taste. Bring to the boil for 5 minutes, then reduce the heat. Create four wells in the mixture and crack an egg into each. Cook for 5 minutes, uncovered, and then 2 minutes, covered, until the whites of the eggs are set but the yolks are still runny.

4 Serve topped with the crumbled feta and chopped parsley.

SmartPoints values per serving 5
SmartPoints values per recipe 19

VEGGIE

Fennel-roasted peppers

Serves 2

Prep time
10 minutes
Cook time
30 minutes

Healthy veg and classic Mediterranean flavours come together in this simple but eye-catching dish.

Ingredients
2 red peppers, halved
and deseeded
1 fennel bulb, cut into
thin wedges
8 cherry tomatoes
1 red onion, cut into
thin wedges
4 garlic cloves, skin on
Calorie controlled
cooking spray
2 sprigs of fresh thyme
1 tablespoon
balsamic vinegar
Handful of rocket, to serve

1 Preheat the oven to 200°C, fan 180°C, gas mark 6. Put the peppers, fennel, tomatoes, onion and garlic in a roasting tray and spray with the cooking spray. Scatter with the thyme and season to taste, then roast for 30 minutes until the vegetables are softened and beginning to char.

2 Remove the garlic cloves and squeeze out the flesh, discarding the papery skin. Combine the soft garlic with the balsamic vinegar.

3 Fill the pepper halves with the other vegetables and serve drizzled with the balsamic dressing and some rocket leaves.

SmartPoints values per serving 1
SmartPoints values per recipe 1

Try this

Save time by buying ready prepared squash – this is also a great way to avoid waste by buying only what you need.

VEGGIE

Creamy Thai vegetable curry

A simple-to-make, light curry featuring all the favourite flavours of Thai cuisine.

Serves 4

Prep time
15 minutes

Cook time
20 minutes

Ingredients
Calorie controlled cooking spray
3 shallots, roughly chopped
350g butternut squash, peeled and cubed
2 tablespoons red or green Thai curry paste (ensure gluten free)
200ml reduced-fat coconut milk
400ml vegetable stock, made from 1 cube (ensure gluten free)
100g green beans, halved
75g pineapple, cut into chunks
150g cherry tomatoes, halved
1 lime, quartered
Chopped fresh coriander, to serve

1 Mist a lidded pan with the cooking spray and cook the shallots for 2-3 minutes until softened. Add the butternut squash and the Thai curry paste. Season to taste and cook for 1 minute, stirring.

2 Pour the coconut milk and the stock into the pan, bring to the boil and then simmer, covered, for 10 minutes.

3 Stir the beans into the curry and cook, uncovered, for 7 minutes, or until the squash and beans are tender. Add the pineapple and tomatoes to the curry and heat through for 1-2 minutes.

4 Ladle the curry into warmed bowls to serve, with a lime wedge to squeeze into the curry, and top with a scattering of fresh coriander.

SmartPoints values per serving 4
SmartPoints values per recipe 16

VEGGIE

Spiced carrot & lentil soup

Serves 6

Prep time
10 minutes

Cook time
30 minutes

Packed with protein-rich lentils, this hearty, warming soup is perfect for feeding a crowd.

Ingredients

Calorie controlled
cooking spray
1 onion, chopped
300g carrots, peeled
and chopped
1 tablespoon garam masala
¼ teaspoon chilli powder
¼ teaspoon ground
turmeric
75g dried red lentils, rinsed
400g tin chopped tomatoes
900ml vegetable stock,
made from 2 cubes (ensure
gluten free)
410g tin green lentils,
rinsed and drained
6 tablespoons 0% fat
natural Greek yogurt
3 tablespoons chopped
fresh coriander

1 Spray a large lidded pan with the cooking spray and fry the onion for 3 minutes.

2 Add the carrots and spices and cook for 1 minute, then tip in the red lentils, tomatoes and stock. Bring to the boil, cover and simmer for 20 minutes, or until the carrots are tender and the red lentils have softened.

3 Blend the soup until smooth using a hand-held blender or a liquidiser. Add the green lentils to the pan and heat through for 2 minutes.

4 Serve the soup topped with a spoonful of the Greek yogurt and a scattering of the chopped coriander.

SmartPoints values per serving 3
SmartPoints values per recipe 18

Quorn fillets with honey & mustard glazed veg

Baby vegetables and protein-rich Quorn add up to a seriously healthy one-pot meal.

Serves 4

Prep time
6 minutes

Cook time
35 minutes

Ingredients
Calorie controlled
cooking spray
8 frozen Quorn fillets
600ml vegetable stock,
made with 1 cube
(ensure gluten free)
400g small new potatoes,
scrubbed and halved
150g Chantenay carrots,
scrubbed and trimmed
Grated zest and
juice of 1 lemon
2 tablespoons
wholegrain mustard
4 teaspoons clear honey
150g baby corn, halved
100g sugar-snap peas

1 Heat a large, lidded, nonstick frying pan over a high heat and mist with the cooking spray. Brown the Quorn fillets for 5-6 minutes, turning to colour evenly. Remove from the pan and set aside.

2 Add the stock and potatoes to the pan. Bring to a simmer, then cover and cook for 10 minutes. Add the carrots and simmer for another 5-8 minutes until the vegetables are tender and the stock is reduced by about two-thirds.

3 Stir in the lemon zest and juice, mustard and honey, then return the Quorn fillets to the pan, along with the baby corn and sugar-snap peas. Simmer for another 5 minutes until the baby corn and sugar snaps are tender, and the sauce is reduced to a sticky glaze, then serve.

SmartPoints values per serving 6
SmartPoints values per recipe 23

Quorn sausage pasta bake

Serves 4

Prep time
10 minutes
Cook time
40 minutes

Enjoy all the meaty flavour and texture of sausages without the saturated fat in this easy all-in-one bake.

Ingredients
Calorie controlled
cooking spray
200g dried spaghetti
6 Quorn sausages,
sliced thickly
400g tin chopped tomatoes
½ teaspoon dried
mixed herbs
¼ teaspoon smoked paprika
3 tablespoons
tomato ketchup
500ml vegetable stock,
made with 1 cube
150g frozen peas
50g fat-reduced mature
vegetarian cheese, grated

1 Preheat the oven to 200°C, fan 180°C, gas mark 6 and put a baking tray on the centre shelf. Mist a 23cm square baking dish with the cooking spray.

2 Roughly break up the spaghetti into the dish and add the Quorn sausages.

3 Combine the chopped tomatoes, mixed herbs, smoked paprika, ketchup and stock. Season to taste, pour into the dish and stir to combine everything.

4 Cover the dish tightly with foil. Put it on the preheated tray and bake for 30-35 minutes, or until the spaghetti is almost tender.

5 Remove the foil, stir in the peas, then scatter the cheese on top. Bake uncovered for a final 5 minutes. Divide between 4 warmed plates or bowls to serve.

SmartPoints values per serving 10
SmartPoints values per recipe 38

Beetroot & pea risotto

Rustle up an edible rainbow with this impressively colourful and healthy twist on an Italian favourite.

Serves 4

Prep time
10 minutes

Cook time
25 minutes

Ingredients

300g cooked beetroot

800ml vegetable stock, made with 1 stock cube (ensure gluten free)

Calorie controlled cooking spray

1 red onion, finely chopped

240g Arborio risotto rice

125g frozen peas

120g 0% fat natural Greek yogurt

Zest of 1 lemon

1 Put half of the beetroot in a food processor with the stock and blitz, reserving the other half to garnish the risotto at the end.

2 Mist a large frying pan with cooking spray. Fry the onion for 5-6 minutes, or until soft. Add the risotto rice and continue to cook for another minute or so.

3 Stir in a ladleful of the beetroot stock mixture until absorbed. Repeat until nearly all the stock has been absorbed and the rice is tender. Stir in the frozen peas and reserved chopped beetroot, then season to taste. Add the final amount of stock and cook for another couple of minutes until the peas and beetroot are warmed through.

4 Mix together the yogurt and lemon zest. Serve the risotto with a spoonful of yogurt on top.

SmartPoints values per serving 7
SmartPoints values per recipe 29

VEGGIE

Curried cauliflower soup

Made from scratch in just 30 minutes, this aromatic, gently spiced soup couldn't be easier.

Ingredients
Calorie controlled
cooking spray
2 onions, chopped
1 tablespoon medium
curry powder
1 small cauliflower,
chopped (include stem
and leaves for flavour)
850ml vegetable stock,
made from 2 cubes
(ensure gluten free)
1 bay leaf
1 teaspoon cumin seeds
Handful of fresh
coriander, chopped

1 Heat a large lidded pan and mist with the cooking spray. Add the onions and cook, stirring, for 4 minutes, until softened, adding a little water if the onions begin to stick. Add the curry powder and cauliflower pieces and stir-fry for 1 minute.

2 Pour over the stock, add the bay leaf and bring to the boil; reduce the heat and cover the pan. Simmer gently for 15 minutes until the cauliflower is tender. Dry-fry the cumin seeds for a minute or so in a small pan, until they release their fragrance.

3 Remove the bay leaf, transfer the soup to a blender (or use a handheld blender) and blitz until smooth. Return the soup to the pan and warm through. Stir through the chopped coriander and season to taste, then serve garnished with the toasted cumin seeds.

SmartPoints values per serving 1
SmartPoints values per recipe 4

VEGGIE

Asparagus & lemon pearl barley risotto

An inspired combo – nutty pearl barley and fresh asparagus with a dash of citrus and a hint of mint.

Serves 4

Prep time
10 minutes

Cook time
40 minutes

Ingredients

250g asparagus, trimmed

Calorie controlled cooking spray

1 onion, finely chopped

2 celery stalks, finely chopped

½ teaspoon fennel seeds

1 garlic clove, crushed

225g pearl barley

1.25 litres hot vegetable stock, made with 2 cubes

Grated zest and juice of 1 lemon

Handful mint leaves, finely chopped, plus extra leaves to garnish

1 Slice the asparagus diagonally, keeping the tips whole. Set aside.

2 Mist a large sauté pan with cooking spray and place over a medium heat. Add the onion, celery and fennel seeds, then cook, stirring, for 4-5 minutes until the vegetables are soft. Add the garlic and cook for a minute more.

3 Stir in the barley. Cook, stirring, for 2 minutes. Gradually pour in 1 litre of the stock, stirring after each addition, making sure all the liquid is absorbed before adding more. This will take about 20 minutes on a low heat.

4 Add the asparagus with the final 250ml of stock and cook for 10-12 minutes, or until the barley is tender.

5 Remove from the heat, stir in the lemon juice and most of the zest, along with the chopped mint. Season to taste. Serve scattered with the mint leaves and remaining zest.

SmartPoints values per serving 7
SmartPoints values per recipe 27

VEGGIE

Beetroot, apple & orange soup

This gloriously simple jewel of a soup not only looks stunning but it's packed full of nutrition and flavour.

Ingredients
½ teaspoon cumin seeds
½ teaspoon fennel seeds
1 tablespoon olive oil
1 onion, thinly sliced
2 sticks celery, chopped
1 carrot, peeled and chopped
2 garlic cloves, chopped
450g raw beetroot, peeled and chopped
1 small apple, peeled, cored and grated
1 litre vegetable stock, made with 1 cube (ensure gluten free)
Juice of ½ orange
2 tablespoons low-fat natural yogurt
2 tablespoons pumpkin seeds, to garnish

1 Toast the cumin and fennel seeds in a dry frying pan over a medium heat for 1-2 minutes, until they begin to release their fragrance, taking care not to burn them. Crush with a pestle and mortar, and set aside.

2 Heat the oil in a large pan, add the onion, celery and carrot and cook for 10 minutes until softened. Add the garlic and the crushed cumin and fennel seeds, then cook for 1 minute. Stir in the beetroot, apple and stock.

3 Bring to a boil, reduce to a simmer and cook for 30 minutes, until the beetroot is tender. Remove from the heat, stir in the orange juice and season to taste. Allow to cool slightly, then blitz in a food processor until smooth (you may need to do this in batches).

4 Return to the pan and reheat, then divide between bowls and serve topped with the yogurt and pumpkin seeds.

SmartPoints values per serving 3
SmartPoints values per recipe 13

Try this

To make this a No Count recipe, swap the naan breads for Weight Watchers Pitta breads.

VEGGIE

Mushroom, spinach & chickpea curry

Rich and satisfying, this classic Indian-style curry is sure to become a family favourite.

Serves 4

Prep time
10 minutes
Cook time
25 minutes

Ingredients
Calorie controlled
cooking spray
1 onion, finely chopped
2 garlic cloves, crushed
2cm-piece fresh ginger,
peeled and grated
1 red chilli, deseeded
and finely chopped
1 teaspoon cumin seeds
1 teaspoon fennel seeds
2 teaspoons garam masala
1 teaspoon ground turmeric
1 teaspoon smoked paprika
1 tablespoon tomato purée
250g mushrooms, sliced
400g tin chickpeas, drained
2 x 400g tins chopped
tomatoes
260g baby leaf spinach
4 Weight Watchers Naan
Breads, warmed, to serve
Fresh coriander, to serve

1 Mist a large pan with cooking spray. Add the onion and cook for 3-4 minutes until beginning to soften, then add the garlic, ginger and chilli. Cook for another minute, add the spices and tomato purée, then cook for 2 minutes until fragrant.

2 Add the mushrooms and sauté for 3-4 minutes until they begin to colour. Stir in the chickpeas and tomatoes, and bring to the boil. Simmer gently for 12-15 minutes until the sauce has thickened slightly. Stir through the spinach to wilt.

3 Serve the curry with a side of naan bread and garnished with a few sprigs of coriander.

SmartPoints values per serving 6
SmartPoints values per recipe 24

VEGGIE

Spicy squash soup

This chunky soup with its warming hit of chilli is just the thing for a cool autumn day.

Serves 4

Prep time
15 minutes
Cook time
35 minutes

Ingredients
Calorie controlled cooking spray
1 large onion, roughly chopped
2 red chillies, deseeded and finely chopped
2 garlic cloves, crushed
½ butternut squash, peeled, deseeded and cubed (about 300g)
2 carrots, peeled and chopped
1.2 litres vegetable stock, made with 2 cubes (ensure gluten free)
Handful fresh coriander leaves, to serve
25g spicy tortilla chips, crushed, to serve
Pinch of chilli powder, to garnish (optional)

1 Mist a large lidded pan with the cooking spray. Sauté the onion for 4-5 minutes until starting to soften. Add the chillies, garlic, squash and carrots, then sauté for a further 4-5 minutes.

2 Pour in the stock, season to taste, then bring to the boil. Reduce the heat, then cover and simmer for 20-25 minutes until the vegetables are tender.

3 Remove from the heat and let cool slightly before blending to a chunky consistency in a blender, or using a hand-held blender.

4 Season to taste, then serve the soup garnished with the coriander, crushed tortillas, chilli powder if using.

SmartPoints values per serving 2
SmartPoints values per recipe 6

Cheat's veggie moussaka

Serves 4

Prep time
15 minutes

Cook time
1 hour

A delicious spin on a Greek classic, this one-pot marvel is just as satisfying as the original version.

Ingredients

Calorie controlled cooking spray
2 large onions, halved and sliced
3 garlic cloves, chopped
400g tin chopped tomatoes
2 tablespoons tomato purée
400ml vegetable stock, made with 1 cube (ensure gluten free)
½ teaspoon ground cinnamon
3 bay leaves
½ teaspoon dried oregano
200g potatoes, peeled, halved and sliced
1 large aubergine, trimmed halved and sliced
350g pack Quorn mince
250g low-fat fromage frais
1 egg
25g reduced-fat feta, crumbled
4 tomatoes, sliced

1 Preheat the oven to 180°C, fan 160°C, gas mark 4. Meanwhile, heat a lidded flameproof and ovenproof dish, over a medium heat, mist with the cooking spray then add the onions and garlic. Stir well, then cover and cook for just under 10 minutes, stirring occasionally and adding a splash of water if they start to stick.

2 Add the tinned tomatoes, purée and stock to the dish, then stir in the cinnamon, bay leaves and oregano. Stir well, then add the potato and aubergine slices.

3 Cover and leave to simmer for 20 minutes, or until the aubergine is soft and the potatoes are tender. Remove from the heat and stir in the Quorn.

4 Beat the fromage frais with the egg and the feta cheese and spread over the Quorn mixture. Arrange the fresh tomato slices on top and season to taste. Bake in the oven for 25 minutes until the topping is set.

SmartPoints values per serving 3
SmartPoints values per recipe 19

VEGGIE

Veggie chilli with baked tortilla chips

Make this nutritious, balanced and super-quick dish with just a few storecupboard essentials.

Serves 4

Prep time
10 minutes

Cook time
25 minutes

Ingredients
Calorie controlled cooking spray
300g pack frozen Quorn mince
395g tin mixed beans in chilli sauce
200g pot fresh salsa
400g tin cherry tomatoes
1-2 teaspoons mild chilli powder
200g mushrooms, sliced
4 Weight Watchers soft flour tortillas

For the side salad
1 carrot, peeled
¼ cucumber
Small handful of fresh coriander or mint
1-2 teaspoons vinegar or lime juice

1 Preheat the oven to 200°C, fan 180°C, gas mark 6. Mist 2 baking sheets with the cooking spray.

2 Tip the Quorn mince into a pan and add the mixed beans, salsa, cherry tomatoes and chilli powder. Stir well and bring to the boil.

3 Add the mushrooms to the pan, stir, then turn down the heat so that the sauce is simmering. Cook for 15 minutes.

4 While the chilli is cooking, prepare the salad by coarsely grating the carrot (do this in your food processor if you prefer). Finely chop the cucumber and coriander or mint and mix everything together with the vinegar or lime juice. Season to taste.

5 Five minutes before the chilli is ready, cut each tortilla into 8 triangles using a pair of scissors. Arrange them on the baking sheets and bake for 3-4 minutes, until crisp. Serve the chilli with the salad and baked tortilla chips.

SmartPoints values per serving 8
SmartPoints values per recipe 33

Try this

You could use different combinations of fruits in this porridge – apples, pears, banana and plums all work well.

Serves 4

Prep time
10 minutes

Cook time
20-25 minutes

Ingredients
100g raspberries
100g blackberries
150g strawberries, hulled and quartered
150g blueberries
150g porridge oats (ensure gluten free)
½ teaspoon ground cinnamon
Pinch of salt
300ml skimmed milk
1 egg
3 tablespoons agave nectar
4 tablespoons 0% fat natural Greek yogurt

 V GF 8 SmartPoints value

VEGGIE

Baked berry porridge

A nourishing, satisfying start to the day that makes the most of colourful summer berries.

1 Preheat the oven to 190°C, fan 170°C, gas mark 5. Put half of the raspberries, blackberries, strawberries and blueberries into a medium baking dish.

2 Mix the oats, cinnamon and salt together in a small bowl, and scatter the mixture over the fruit.

3 Whisk the milk, egg and agave nectar together in a jug and pour it over the oats and fruit. Scatter the rest of the fruit over the top and bake for 20-25 minutes until the liquid is absorbed and the fruit is soft. Serve the berry porridge warm with the Greek yogurt.

SmartPoints values per serving 8
SmartPoints values per recipe 31

Poultry & fish

Poached chicken with spring vegetables

A beautiful spring hot-pot with delicate, fresh flavours, this is a dish all the family will enjoy.

Ingredients
1 litre chicken stock,
made with 1 stock cube
(ensure gluten free)
4 x 150g skinless and
boneless chicken breast
fillets, cut into 2cm strips
350g new potatoes, halved
2 fresh bay leaves
3 whole peppercorns
Zest and juice of 1 lemon
200g baby carrots,
halved lengthways
150g baby leeks, trimmed
and cut into 2-3cm pieces
100g asparagus tips, cut
into 2-3cm pieces
400g tin artichoke hearts in
water, drained, rinsed and
quartered
100g frozen peas
2 tablespoons chopped
fresh flat-leaf parsley

1 Bring the chicken stock to a simmer in a large pan or casserole dish.

2 Add the chicken, potatoes, bay leaves, peppercorns and lemon zest, and simmer for 10 minutes. Add the carrots and leeks, and cook for another 5 minutes, then stir in the asparagus, artichokes and peas.

3 Cook for about 3 minutes or until the asparagus is just tender. Stir through the parsley and lemon juice, then serve.

SmartPoints values per serving 4
SmartPoints values per recipe 16

Serves 2

Prep time
10 minutes
Cook time
50 minutes

POULTRY

All-in-one roast chicken

This tender chicken and veg bake is flavoured with Mediterranean herbs and served with a yogurt sauce.

Ingredients

4 x 125g skinless chicken legs, visible fat removed
4 x 175g potatoes, cut into large chunks
2 red onions, each cut into 6 wedges
4 carrots, peeled and cut into large chunks
8 garlic cloves, unpeeled
1 orange, zested, and flesh cut into 8 chunks
Pinch of dried chilli flakes
Sprig of fresh rosemary
2 fresh bay leaves
1 teaspoon dried thyme
Calorie controlled cooking spray
250g 0% fat Greek yogurt
1 tablespoon chopped fresh parsley

1 Preheat the oven to 220°C, fan 200°C, gas mark 7. Put the chicken, vegetables, garlic and orange chunks in a large roasting tin, big enough to fit everything in a single layer. Add the chilli flakes and rosemary sprig, and tuck the bay leaves in under the chicken and vegetables. Sprinkle with the dried thyme and pour in 200ml of water. Mist everything with the cooking spray and season well.

2 Roast for 10 minutes, then turn down the oven to 200°C, fan 180°C, gas mark 6. Cook for a further 30-40 minutes, until the chicken and vegetables are tender and starting to turn golden.

3 Remove from the oven and transfer the chicken and vegetables to a serving platter, discarding the bay leaves and rosemary and setting aside the garlic cloves.

4 To make the yogurt and garlic sauce, squeeze the flesh from the cloves into a bowl and mash thoroughly. Stir in the yogurt, orange zest and parsley. Season to taste and serve with the chicken and roasted vegetables.

SmartPoints values per serving 8
SmartPoints values per recipe 30

Cook's tip

Serve this with 120g cooked brown rice per person, for an extra 4 SmartPoints per serving.

Serves 4

Prep time
20 minutes
Cook time
25 minutes

Ingredients
Calorie controlled
cooking spray
2 onions, chopped
1 red pepper, deseeded
and sliced
2 garlic cloves, crushed
5cm-piece fresh root
ginger, grated
600g skinless boneless
chicken breasts, cubed
1 green pepper, deseeded
and sliced
1 green chilli, deseeded
and sliced into thin rounds,
plus extra sliced chilli
to garnish
1 tablespoon medium curry
powder (ensure gluten free)
1 teaspoon cumin seeds
400g passata

POULTRY

Chicken jalfrezi

Green chilli is a vital ingredient in jalfrezi – add more or less, depending on how spicy you like it.

1 Heat a lidded saucepan over a medium heat. Mist with the cooking spray and fry the onions for 5 minutes. Add the red pepper, garlic and ginger, mist again with the cooking spray, and fry for another 3 minutes until the vegetables have softened.

2 Using a hand-held blender, purée the onion and veg mixture with 4 tablespoons of water until smooth, then remove the mixture from the pan and set aside until ready to use.

3 Return the pan to the heat, spray with the cooking spray, and stir-fry the chicken for 5 minutes until browned in places. Add the green pepper and chilli, then stir-fry for another 2 minutes.

4 Return the onion and veg mixture to the pan and add the curry powder, cumin seeds and passata. Stir, bring to the boil, then reduce the heat and simmer, part-covered, for 10 minutes, until the sauce has reduced and thickened and the chicken has cooked through. Season to taste and serve with the extra chilli.

SmartPoints values per serving 2
SmartPoints values per recipe 8

POULTRY

Cajun chicken

A tasty, spicy chicken and rice dish that's baked in the oven and taken straight to the table.

Serves 4

Prep time
15 minutes

Cook time
1 hour
15 minutes

Ingredients
Calorie controlled
cooking spray
4 x 150g skinless boneless
chicken breast fillets,
cut into chunks
1 onion, thinly sliced
1 red and 1 yellow pepper,
deseeded and finely sliced
4 garlic cloves, thinly sliced
1 tablespoon chopped fresh
thyme, plus a
few sprigs to garnish
2-3 teaspoons Cajun
seasoning
200g white rice
150g green beans
1 tablespoon tomato purée
600ml hot chicken stock,
made with 1 cube
(ensure gluten free)

1 Preheat the oven to 200°C, fan 180°C, gas mark 6. Mist a large, shallow, flameproof casserole with the cooking spray, add the chicken and cook for 5 minutes until golden.

2 Add the onion, peppers and garlic, then cook for 5 minutes. Add the chopped thyme and Cajun seasoning, then cook for 2 minutes.

3 Stir in the rice and beans. In a jug, mix the tomato purée into the stock then pour over the chicken mixture. Cover then transfer to the oven. Bake for 1 hour, stirring occasionally.

4 Allow to stand for a couple of minutes then serve garnished with the thyme sprigs.

SmartPoints values per serving 7
SmartPoints values per recipe 28

Cook's tip

Turkey is a good source of protein, so it keeps you feeling full. Turkey breast is also very lean, with less fat than chicken breast.

POULTRY

Turkey & sweet potato chilli

Liven up a conventional chilli con carne with colourful veg to make it a complete, one-pot meal.

Serves 4

Prep time
10 minutes

Cook time
45 minutes

Ingredients

Calorie controlled cooking spray
500g turkey breast mince
1 onion, diced
2-3 garlic cloves, chopped
250g sweet potato, cubed (skin on)
1 teaspoon hot chilli powder
395g tin red kidney beans in chilli sauce
400g tin chopped tomatoes
300g baby leaf spinach

1 Heat a wide, nonstick sauté pan and mist with cooking spray. Add the turkey, season, then cook over a high heat for 5-6 minutes, breaking the mince up with a wooden spoon, until there is no pink meat left. Tip onto a plate and set aside.

2 Mist the pan with spray and add the onion, garlic and sweet potato, with a splash of water. Cook over a medium-high heat for 15 minutes, stirring occasionally and adding more water to prevent sticking, until the vegetables are tender.

3 Stir through the chilli powder, kidney beans and tomatoes. Fill the empty bean tin with water and pour into the pan. Return the cooked mince to the pan, stir to combine, and simmer for 15-20 minutes.

4 Stir in the spinach to wilt and serve seasoned with freshly ground black pepper.

SmartPoints values per serving 4
SmartPoints values per recipe 25

Pot roast chicken with fennel & potatoes

Serves 2

Prep time
10 minutes
Cook time
30 minutes

For a Sunday roast with none of the stress, try this easy one-pot version – it even includes the gravy!

Ingredients
Calorie controlled cooking spray
1 x 165g skinless chicken breast, cut into 4 pieces
2 x 45g skinless chicken thighs, cut into chunks
1 tablespoon plain flour
1 tablespoon tomato purée
300ml hot chicken stock, made with 1 stock cube
300g new potatoes, halved
½ whole celeriac, peeled and finely diced
2 fennel bulbs, trimmed and cut into wedges
2 carrots, peeled and cut into thin wedges
Small bunch of fresh thyme sprigs, plus extra to garnish

1 Heat a flameproof, lidded casserole over a high heat and mist with cooking spray. When hot, add the chicken and cook, turning, until golden all over.

2 Meanwhile, mix together the flour and tomato purée to form a paste. Stir the paste into the hot chicken stock until combined, then pour over the chicken. Add the vegetables and thyme and season to taste.

3 Bring to the boil, then cover. Reduce the heat and simmer for 20 minutes until the chicken is cooked, the vegetables are tender and the sauce has thickened. Serve garnished with the extra thyme.

SmartPoints values per serving 8
SmartPoints values per recipe 16

Turkey stir-fry

Serves 4

Prep time
15 minutes
Cook time
15 minutes

Full of Asian-inspired flavours, this easy stir-fry
is quick to cook and on the table in half an hour.

Ingredients
500g diced turkey breast
Calorie controlled
cooking spray
4 shallots, sliced
4cm-piece fresh root
ginger, shredded
3 garlic cloves, sliced
1 red chilli, sliced
200g broccoli, broken into
small florets
150ml chicken stock,
made with ½ cube
(ensure gluten free)
200g pak choi, separated
into leaves and stems,
chopped roughly
200g beansprouts, rinsed
Juice of 1 lime
1½ tablespoons Thai fish
sauce (ensure gluten free)

1 Season the turkey and mist a wok or large nonstick frying pan
with the cooking spray. Stir-fry the turkey for 5 minutes over
a high heat. Transfer to a plate.

2 Tip the shallots, ginger, garlic and chilli into the wok or
pan and stir-fry for 2 minutes. Add the broccoli and
4 tablespoons of the stock, and steam-fry for 3 minutes,
adding another 2 tablespoons of stock as the first addition
of stock evaporates.

3 Add the pak choi stems and 2 tablespoons of stock to the
wok or pan and cook for a further 2 minutes. Finally, add the
pak choi leaves, beansprouts, browned turkey and the rest of
the stock, along with the lime juice and fish sauce. Stir-fry for
2–3 minutes then serve immediately.

SmartPoints values per serving 2
SmartPoints values per recipe 7

Kung Pao chicken

Forget your Chinese takeaway – this healthier version of the classic dish is every bit as good.

Serves 4

Prep time
20 minutes,
plus marinating

Cook time
20 minutes

Ingredients
650g skinless chicken
breast, cut into chunks
3 tablespoons soy sauce
(ensure gluten free)
3 tablespoons rice
wine vinegar
½ teaspoon Szechuan
peppercorns
Calorie controlled
cooking spray
2 garlic cloves, sliced
2cm-piece fresh ginger,
peeled and grated
2 tablespoons hoisin sauce
(ensure gluten free)
1 teaspoon cornflour
½ teaspoon red chilli flakes
6 spring onions, sliced
3 carrots, peeled
2 courgettes
1 tablespoon sesame oil
Handful fresh coriander,
roughly chopped

1 Put the chicken in a shallow dish. Mix together 2 tablespoons of the soy sauce and 1 tablespoon of the rice wine vinegar, and pour over the chicken. Cover with cling film and leave to marinate in the fridge for at least 1 hour.

2 Toast the Szechuan peppercorns in a dry wok or frying pan over a medium heat for 2 minutes, then crush with a pestle and mortar and set aside.

3 Mist the wok or pan with cooking spray and fry the chicken over a medium-high heat for 8-10 minutes. Add the garlic and ginger and cook for 2 minutes.

4 Whisk together the remaining soy sauce, 1 tablespoon of the rice wine vinegar, the hoisin sauce, cornflour, chilli flakes and Szechuan pepper, then pour into the wok. Cook for 1 minute then add the spring onions.

5 Use a vegetable peeler to slice the carrot and courgettes into thin ribbons and put them in a bowl. Whisk together the remaining rice wine vinegar and the sesame oil, and drizzle over the veg. Add half the coriander and toss to combine. Serve the chicken and veg garnished with the remaining coriander.

SmartPoints values per serving 5
SmartPoints values per recipe 18

Tex-Mex turkey

This colourful dish is full of healthy veg and topped with crushed tortilla chips and crème fraîche.

Serves 4

Prep time
15 minutes
Cook time
25 minutes

Ingredients
Calorie controlled
cooking spray
1 red onion, chopped
1 red pepper, deseeded
and diced
1 courgette, diced
1 tablespoon ground cumin
1 teaspoon smoked paprika,
plus extra to garnish
¼ teaspoon chilli powder
2 garlic cloves, crushed
500g turkey breast, cubed
400g tin chopped tomatoes
150ml chicken stock,
made with ½ cube
(ensure gluten free)
198g tin sweetcorn, drained
4 tablespoons reduced-fat
crème fraîche
60g tortilla chips, crushed
(ensure gluten free)

1 Mist a lidded flameproof casserole dish with the cooking spray. Fry the onion, pepper and courgette over a high heat for 3 minutes, stirring.

2 Add the spices, garlic and turkey, and cook for 2 minutes, then add the tomatoes, stock and sweetcorn. Season to taste and simmer, covered, for 20 minutes.

3 Serve the turkey mixture ladled into bowls, topped with a spoonful of crème fraîche, a sprinkling of paprika and the crushed tortilla chips.

SmartPoints values per serving 7
SmartPoints values per recipe 29

Chicken & barley stew

Serves 2

Prep time
10 minutes
Cook time
35 minutes

A traditional-style one-pot dish that's packed with flavour and makes a great winter warmer.

Ingredients
400ml vegetable stock,
made with 1 cube
1 bay leaf
20g pearl barley, washed
1 celery stick, chopped
1 carrot, peeled and
chopped
1 leek, trimmed
and chopped
120g cooked skinless,
boneless chicken breast
Finely chopped fresh
chives, to garnish

1 Put the stock and bay leaf in a lidded pan and bring to the boil. Add the pearl barley, bring back to the boil, cover and simmer for 15 minutes. Add the vegetables, return to the boil, then cover and simmer for a further 15 minutes or until the pearl barley is just tender.

2 Shred the chicken breast and add to the pan to warm through for a couple of minutes. Season to taste and serve in large bowls, garnished with chopped chives.

SmartPoints values per serving 3
SmartPoints values per recipe 5

Keralan coconut fish curry

Serves 4

Prep time
10 minutes
Cook time
10 minutes

This fragrant fish curry has a coconut milk base, which gives it a luxuriously creamy taste.

Ingredients
1 small onion, roughly chopped
3 garlic cloves
2cm-piece fresh ginger, sliced
1 tablespoon hot curry powder (ensure gluten free)
Grated zest and juice of ½ lime
300ml reduced-fat coconut milk
Calorie controlled cooking spray
450g firm white fish fillets, cubed
200g cherry tomatoes, halved
100g baby leaf spinach

1 Put the onion, garlic, ginger, curry powder, lime zest and juice in a small food processor with 2 tablespoons of the coconut milk and whiz to a paste (or use a hand-held blender).

2 Mist a nonstick saucepan with the cooking spray and add the spice paste. Fry for 4-5 minutes to cook out the raw flavours. Add the fish to the pan and turn gently to coat in the spice paste.

3 Pour the rest of the coconut milk into the pan and stir in the tomatoes. Bring to the boil and simmer gently for 5 minutes until the fish is cooked but not falling apart.

4 Remove from the heat and stir in the spinach, to wilt in the heat of the sauce. Season to taste. Ladle into warmed bowls to serve.

SmartPoints values per serving 5
SmartPoints values per recipe 21

FISH

Serves 4

Classic seafood stew

Prep time
20 minutes
Cook time
30 minutes

Succulent seafood, peppers, tomatoes and new potatoes come together in this simple, delicious stew.

Ingredients
1 tablespoon olive oil
1 onion, thinly sliced
3 garlic cloves, chopped
1 fennel bulb, sliced
thinly and fronds reserved
Pinch of dried chilli flakes
1 red and 1 yellow pepper,
deseeded and sliced
500ml vegetable or chicken
stock, made with 1 stock
cube (ensure gluten free)
400g tin chopped tomatoes
250g new potatoes, sliced
Grated zest of ½ orange
200g firm skinless white
fish fillet, cubed
350g seafood selection,
defrosted if frozen

1 Heat the olive oil in a large, flameproof, lidded casserole and cook the onion, garlic and fennel for 4 minutes, uncovered, over a medium heat, stirring occasionally.

2 Add the chilli flakes, peppers and 100ml of the stock. Cover and cook for 5 minutes until the vegetables start to soften.

3 Tip the tomatoes into the casserole with the rest of the stock, the sliced potatoes and the orange zest. Season to taste, bring to the boil and cook, covered, for 15 minutes, or until the potatoes are tender.

4 Stir the fish and seafood mix into the casserole and cook gently for 4–5 minutes until the fish is just starting to flake and the seafood is heated through.

5 Ladle into deep bowls and serve with the fennel fronds scattered over the top.

SmartPoints values per serving 4
SmartPoints values per recipe 16

Cook's tip

It's important to use paella rice in this dish because it holds its shape and won't clump together like other types of rice.

Serves 4

Prep time
10 minutes
Cook time
40 minutes

Ingredients
Calorie controlled
cooking spray
1 onion, finely sliced
1 red pepper, deseeded
and sliced (optional)
2 garlic cloves,
finely chopped
½ teaspoon smoked paprika
Pinch saffron, soaked
in 2 teaspoons cold water
150g paella rice
500ml chicken stock,
made with 1 cube
(ensure gluten free)
300g cooked king prawns,
tails left on
200g raw squid rings
100g frozen garden peas
Handful fresh flat-leaf
parsley, leaves
picked and chopped
1 lemon, cut into wedges

FISH

Seafood paella

A Spanish classic flavoured with paprika and saffron, and packed with tasty seafood and veg.

1 Mist a large lidded frying pan with cooking spray and cook the onion for 5 minutes over a medium heat. Add the pepper, if using, and cook for another 5 minutes.

2 Stir in the garlic, paprika, saffron and rice, and cook for 1 minute before pouring in the stock. Bring to a boil, turn down to a simmer, cover and cook for 15 minutes.

3 Add the prawns, squid rings, peas and half the parsley to the pan. Stir then cover and continue to cook for 5 minutes. Remove the lid and cook for a final 3-4 minutes to absorb the last of the stock.

4 Season to taste and garnish with the remaining parsley, then serve with the lemon wedges on the side.

SmartPoints values per serving 5
SmartPoints values per recipe 22

FISH

Serves 4

Mediterranean cod bake

Prep time
10 minutes
Cook time
25 minutes

A perfect dish for entertaining, you can prepare this ahead of time and bake it at the last minute.

Ingredients
Calorie controlled
cooking spray
1 yellow and 1 green
pepper, deseeded
and sliced
2 garlic cloves, sliced
400g tin chopped tomatoes
3 heaped tablespoons
shredded fresh basil
4 x 125g skinless
cod fillets
125g reduced-fat
mozzarella, torn
200g sugar snap peas

1 Preheat the oven to 200°C, fan 180°C, gas mark 6. Mist a shallow ovenproof casserole dish with cooking spray.

2 Heat the casserole dish over a gentle heat, add the peppers and garlic and cook for around 5 minutes until browned and starting to soften. Add the tomatoes and basil to the dish, season to taste and allow to simmer for 3-4 minutes until slightly thickened.

3 Remove from the heat, put the cod fillets in the sauce and scatter the torn mozzarella over the top. Bake for around 15 minutes until the fish is cooked.

4 While the fish is cooking, microwave the sugar snaps with 2 tablespoons of water in a covered microwave-proof dish on high for 1 minute. Serve with the cod bake.

SmartPoints values per serving 3
SmartPoints values per recipe 10

FISH

Spicy prawn laksa

Serves 4

Prep time
5 minutes
Cook time
15 minutes

A Malaysian-style soup with a spicy kick. Using ready-cooked noodles keeps it really simple.

Ingredients

2 teaspoons olive oil
5 spring onions, chopped
1 garlic clove, chopped
2cm-piece fresh ginger, chopped
1 red chilli, deseeded and chopped
3 tablespoons laksa paste
150ml reduced-fat coconut milk
1 litre chicken stock, made with 1 stock cube (ensure gluten free)
1 courgette, sliced
1 red pepper, sliced
300g raw prawns, shelled
100g mange tout, halved
100g frozen peas
300g ready-cooked rice noodles
Juice of 1 lime
2 tablespoons soy sauce
2 teaspoons fish sauce
Fresh coriander, to garnish

1 Heat the oil in a large wok or frying pan and fry the spring onions, garlic, ginger and chilli for 2 minutes.

2 Stir in the laksa paste and fry for 2 minutes, then pour in the coconut milk and the stock.

3 Bring to a gentle simmer, then add the courgette, pepper and prawns. Cook for 4 minutes then add the mange tout, peas and rice noodles. Simmer for a further 2 minutes. Season with the lime juice and soy and fish sauces.

4 Ladle into bowls and serve garnished with the coriander.

SmartPoints values per serving 6
SmartPoints values per recipe 24

Meat

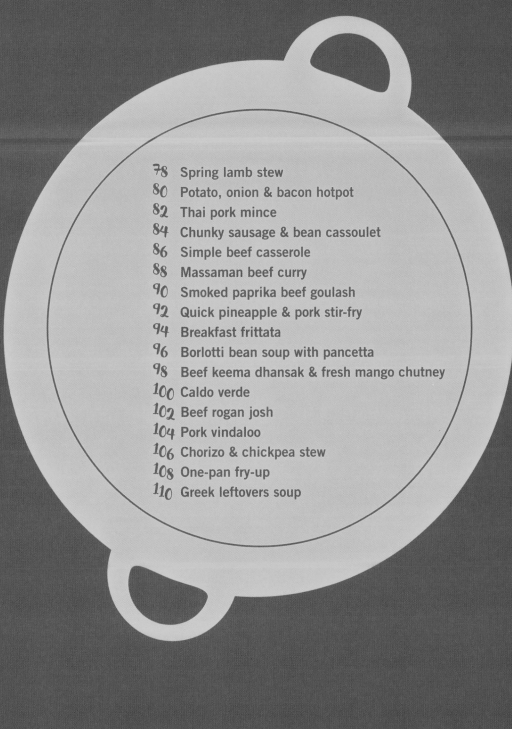

MEAT

Spring lamb stew

This colourful and chunky stew brings the
best flavours of spring together in one pot.

Ingredients
Calorie controlled
cooking spray
400g lean lamb leg steaks,
cut into chunks
8 shallots, halved
8 baby leeks, trimmed
cut into 3-4 pieces
400g small carrots,
halved lengthways
400g small new
potatoes, scrubbed
1.2 litres vegetable stock
made from 2 cubes
(ensure gluten free)
2 tablespoons chopped
fresh parsley
100g fresh or frozen peas
2 tablespoons cornflour

1 Mist a large heavy-based pan with the cooking spray. Add
the lamb, a handful at a time, and cook over a high heat
until sealed and browned – about 3-4 minutes.

2 Add the shallots, leeks, carrots, new potatoes, stock and
1 tablespoon of parsley. Bring to the boil, then reduce the
heat and simmer, covered, for 45 minutes.

3 Add the peas to the stew, stir, and season to taste, then cook
for a further 5 minutes.

4 Blend the cornflour with 3 tablespoons of cold water and
add to the stew, stirring until thickened. Add the remaining
parsley, then ladle into 4 warmed bowls and serve.

SmartPoints values per serving 9
SmartPoints values per recipe 37

MEAT

Potato, onion & bacon hotpot

Serves 4

Prep time
20 minutes
Cook time
1 hour 15 minutes

Who could resist this mouthwatering dish of layered potatoes and onions topped with tasty bacon?

Ingredients
1kg floury potatoes,
peeled and thinly sliced
2 large onions,
thinly sliced
1 litre chicken or
vegetable stock made
from 2 cubes
(ensure gluten free)
8 slices Weight Watchers
Extra Trimmed
Unsmoked Back Bacon
A few sprigs of
fresh thyme

1 Preheat the oven to 190°C, fan 170°C, gas mark 5.

2 Arrange the potato and onion slices in alternate layers in a 2.5 litre baking dish or casserole dish, seasoning each layer as you go, and finishing with a layer of potatoes. Pour the stock over the potato and onion slices.

3 Transfer to the oven and bake, uncovered, for 1 hour, or until the potatoes are tender. Arrange the bacon slices and thyme sprigs on top of the hotpot and bake for another 15 minutes. The top layer of the potatoes and the bacon should be crisp.

4 Divide between 4 warmed plates and serve.

SmartPoints values per serving 8
SmartPoints values per recipe 30

MEAT

Thai pork mince

Serves 4

Prep time
10 minutes
Cook time
30 minutes

Ingredients
**Calorie controlled
cooking spray
500g extra-lean pork mince
1 red chilli, deseeded and
finely chopped
3 garlic cloves, crushed
1 lemongrass stalk,
finely chopped
1 red pepper, deseeded
and chopped
150g mushrooms, quartered
1 tablespoon Thai fish
sauce (ensure gluten free)
300ml chicken stock made
from ½ cube (ensure
gluten free)
150g sugar snap
peas, sliced lengthways
Juice of ½ lime
150g beansprouts, rinsed
Chopped fresh coriander,
to garnish
Lime wedges, to serve**

You can also try this dish with lean turkey mince or wrapped into crunchy iceberg lettuce leaves.

1 Mist a large nonstick saucepan or wok with the cooking spray and brown the mince over a high heat for 5 minutes, stirring to break it up.

2 Add the chilli, garlic, lemongrass, red pepper and mushrooms and cook for 2 minutes.

3 Add the fish sauce and stock. Season to taste and bring to the boil. Cover and simmer the mince mixture for 15 minutes.

4 Add in the sugar snap peas and cook for 5 minutes. Stir in the lime juice and beansprouts, then ladle the Thai pork mince into bowls. Garnish with the coriander and serve with lime wedges.

SmartPoints values per serving 4
SmartPoints values per recipe 16

Cook's tip

This is a great recipe for batch cooking – make double and freeze for later. You could use veggie sausages if you prefer.

Serves 4

Prep time
10 minutes
Cook time
30 minutes

MEAT

Chunky sausage & bean cassoulet

An easy-peasy crowd-pleaser with lots of lovely chunky veg, butter beans and reduced-fat sausages.

Ingredients
Calorie controlled cooking spray
6 Weight Watchers Premium Pork Sausages
2 leeks, trimmed and sliced
400g tin chopped tomatoes
1 teaspoon dried mixed herbs
1 tablespoon tomato purée
½ chicken or vegetable stock cube, crumbled (ensure gluten free)
400g tin butter beans, drained and rinsed

1 Put a large lidded pan over a medium heat, mist with the cooking spray and add the sausages. Cook the sausages until browned. Remove from the pan and, when cool enough to handle, cut each into 3 pieces and set aside. They do not need to be cooked all the way through at this point.

2 Mist the pan again with the cooking spray, add the leeks and cook for 2 minutes until they start to soften. Add the tomatoes, herbs, tomato purée and stock cube. Half-fill the empty tomato tin with water and add to the pan. Season to taste.

3 Bring to the boil and add the sausage pieces. Reduce the heat, cover the pan and cook for 20 minutes.

4 Stir in the butter beans, cook for a further 5 minutes and serve in warmed bowls.

SmartPoints values per serving 3
SmartPoints values per recipe 13

Try this

You could serve the casserole with 100g boiled new potatoes per person, for an extra 2 SmartPoints per serving.

Serves 6

Prep time
20 minutes
Cook time
1 hour 35 minutes

Ingredients
Calorie controlled cooking spray
1 onion, roughly chopped
2 celery sticks, roughly chopped
4 carrots, roughly chopped
2 garlic cloves, crushed
1 tablespoon plain flour
1 teaspoon ground cinnamon
500g cubed lean beef stewing steak
2 tablespoons tomato purée
3 tablespoons balsamic vinegar
125ml red wine
400ml beef stock, made with 1 stock cube
¼ teaspoon dried thyme
Fresh thyme, to garnish

MEAT

Simple beef casserole

Coating the beef in cinnamon adds a warm, mildly spicy note to this easy-going casserole.

1 Preheat the oven to 150°C, fan 130°C, gas mark 2.

2 Mist a lidded flameproof casserole with the cooking spray and brown the onion, celery and carrots over a high heat for about 4 minutes. Add the garlic and cook for 1 minute.

3 Meanwhile, combine the flour and cinnamon in a large bowl and add some seasoning. Toss the beef in the spiced flour to coat. Tip the beef and any extra flour into the casserole along with the tomato purée and balsamic vinegar. Pour in the red wine and stock, and sprinkle in the dried thyme.

4 Bring the casserole to the boil, cover with a lid and put in the oven to cook for 1½ hours or until the meat and vegetables are tender. Ladle into bowls and garnish with fresh thyme sprigs to serve.

SmartPoints values per serving 3
SmartPoints values per recipe 17

86

Massaman beef curry

Serves 4

Prep time
15 minutes
Cook time
25 minutes

Originating in Thailand, this hearty curry is wonderfully rich with layers of incredible flavour.

Ingredients
Calorie controlled cooking spray
4 shallots, sliced
400g potatoes, peeled and cubed
1 teaspoon curry powder
2 tablespoons red Thai curry paste (ensure gluten free)
200ml reduced-fat coconut milk
1 tablespoon Thai fish sauce (ensure gluten free)
400ml beef stock made with 1 cube (ensure gluten free)
1 cinnamon stick
100g green beans, trimmed
300g lean beef escalopes, cut into strips
25g peanuts, chopped
½ red chilli, finely sliced

1 Mist a large lidded saucepan with the cooking spray, add the shallots and stir-fry for 2 minutes.

2 Add the potatoes, curry powder and Thai curry paste and cook, stirring, for 1 minute.

3 Pour in the coconut milk, fish sauce and beef stock. Add the cinnamon stick and simmer, covered, for 10 minutes.

4 Add the green beans to the pan and cook for a further 5 minutes before adding the beef. Cook gently for 3 minutes or until the beef is just cooked through but still tender. Remove the cinnamon stick.

5 Ladle the curry into bowls and sprinkle the chopped peanuts and chilli on top, then serve.

GF — SmartPoints value **11**

SmartPoints values per serving 11
SmartPoints values per recipe 45

Smoked paprika beef goulash

Paprika is a mainstay of Hungarian cooking and it's the starring flavour in this nation's most famous dish.

Serves 4

Prep time
20 minutes

Cook time
1 hour 45 minutes

Ingredients

500g lean braising steak, cubed
Calorie controlled cooking spray
2 onions, sliced
2 garlic cloves, crushed
½ tablespoon smoked paprika
400g tin chopped tomatoes
300ml beef stock made with ½ cube (ensure gluten free)
1 red pepper, deseeded and sliced
1 green pepper, deseeded and sliced
410g tin butter beans, drained and rinsed

1 Preheat the oven to 150°C, fan 130°C, gas mark 2.

2 Season the steak and mist a lidded flameproof casserole with the cooking spray. Brown the steak in 2 batches, transferring the meat to a plate after it is browned.

3 Mist the casserole with a little more cooking spray and cook the onions for 5 minutes. Stir in the garlic and smoked paprika and cook for 1 minute, then add the tomatoes, beef stock and browned beef. Season to taste, bring to a simmer, then cover and cook in the oven for 1 hour.

4 Stir the peppers and butter beans into the stew, pushing them down into the liquid, then replace the lid and cook for a further 30 minutes, or until the meat is tender.

SmartPoints values per serving 5
SmartPoints values per recipe 19

MEAT

Quick pineapple & pork stir-fry

Turn up the heat on this classic sweet and sour combo with ginger, chilli and Chinese five spice.

Serves 4

Prep time
15 minutes

Cook time
15 minutes

Ingredients

1 teaspoon Chinese five spice powder
400g lean pork strips
200g canned pineapple chunks in natural juice
1 tablespoon cornflour
2 tablespoons cider vinegar
2 tablespoons gluten free soy sauce
2 tablespoons gluten free tomato ketchup
Calorie controlled cooking spray
1 onion, sliced
3 mixed peppers, deseeded and cut into chunks
1 red chilli, deseeded and sliced
2 garlic cloves, sliced
2cm-piece fresh ginger, shredded
200g pak choi, chopped

1 Sprinkle the Chinese five spice powder into a bowl with some seasoning. Add the pork and turn to coat. Set aside.

2 Drain the pineapple and reserve 30ml of the juice. Set aside the pineapple and pour the reserved juice into a jug, then whisk in the cornflour, cider vinegar, soy sauce, and tomato ketchup. Add 250ml cold water and set aside.

3 Mist a wok or nonstick frying pan with the cooking spray and stir-fry the pork for 3 minutes over a high heat, until just cooked through. Transfer to a plate.

4 Stir-fry the onion and peppers for 3-4 minutes before adding the chilli, garlic, ginger and pak choi. Cook for 2 minutes, stirring.

5 Return the pork to the wok or pan and add the pineapple chunks. Give the sauce a stir and pour it into the pan. Cook for 2 minutes, stirring, as the sauce thickens to make sure that everything is well coated. Serve immediately.

SmartPoints values per serving 6
SmartPoints values per recipe 22

MEAT

Breakfast frittata

Breakfast, lunch or dinner, this cracking egg-based feast is the perfect dish for any mealtime!

Serves 4

Prep time
15 minutes

Cook time
30 minutes

Ingredients
Calorie controlled
cooking spray
200g Weight Watchers
Premium Pork Sausages,
cut into small chunks
1 onion, finely chopped
250g chestnut mushrooms,
thinly sliced
225g cooked
potatoes, diced
150g cherry
tomatoes, halved
6 eggs

1 Heat a 22cm nonstick ovenproof frying pan over a medium heat; mist with cooking spray. Add the sausages and cook for 5 minutes until golden all over, then transfer to a plate.

2 Add the onion to the pan and cook for 5 minutes. Add the mushrooms and cook for a further 6-8 minutes or until the mushrooms are golden.

3 Return the sausages to the pan along with the cooked potatoes and half the cherry tomatoes. Season and give everything a stir. Whisk the eggs and cheese together in a measuring jug, season, then pour into the pan. Arrange the remaining cherry tomatoes on top and cook for 5 minutes or until the eggs are beginning to set. Meanwhile, preheat the grill to medium.

4 Transfer the pan to the grill and cook for 2-3 minutes or until the top is set and just golden.

SmartPoints values per serving 7
SmartPoints values per recipe 26

MEAT

Borlotti bean soup with pancetta

Serves 4

Prep time
15 minutes
Cook time
40 minutes

A simple Italian-inspired bean soup that's packed with lots of lovely rich and hearty flavours.

Ingredients
Calorie controlled cooking spray
1 large red onion, chopped
2 celery sticks, chopped
1 large carrot, peeled and diced
150g potato, diced
1 fennel bulb, trimmed and finely chopped
100g cubed pancetta
3 garlic cloves, chopped
Sprig of rosemary
1 fresh bay leaf
410g tin borlotti beans, drained and rinsed
1 large courgette, chopped
900ml chicken stock, made with 2 cubes (ensure gluten free)
30g Parmesan, grated, to serve

1 Mist a large pan with cooking spray and sauté the onion, celery, carrot, potato, fennel, pancetta and garlic for 15 minutes or so, until the veg is soft and golden. Add the rosemary, bay leaf, beans, courgette and stock, season and simmer for 25 minutes.

2 Using a potato masher, crush the veg slightly. Serve the soup seasoned with freshly ground black pepper and topped with grated Parmesan.

SmartPoints values per serving 8
SmartPoints values per recipe 31

Beef keema dhansak & fresh mango chutney

Why bother with shop-bought mango chutney when this accompaniment is so easy to make?

Serves 6

Prep time
20 minutes

Cook time
40 minutes

Ingredients
Calorie controlled
cooking spray
500g extra-lean beef mince
1 onion, finely chopped
1 tablespoon medium curry
powder (ensure gluten free)
2 garlic cloves, crushed
400g tin chopped tomatoes
100g dried red lentils
400ml beef stock made
with 1 cube (ensure
gluten free)
100g young leaf spinach

For the mango chutney
1 large ripe mango, peeled,
stone removed and
flesh finely chopped
½ red chilli, deseeded and
finely chopped
Zest and juice of ½ lime
3 tablespoons chopped
fresh coriander

1 Mist a large flameproof lidded casserole with cooking spray. Brown the mince and onion together for 5 minutes over a high heat, stirring frequently to break the mince up. Add the curry powder and garlic and cook for 2 minutes.

2 Mix in the tomatoes, then rinse the lentils in a sieve under cold running water, and add them to the casserole, along with the stock. Bring to the boil, then cover and reduce to a simmer for 25 minutes or until the lentils are soft.

3 Stir in the spinach, adjust the seasoning to taste and cook for a further 5 minutes.

4 While the curry is cooking, simply combine the mango chutney ingredients in a bowl and set aside for the flavours to infuse.

5 Ladle the curry into warmed bowls and serve topped with the fresh mango chutney.

SmartPoints values per serving 4
SmartPoints values per recipe 23

MEAT

Caldo verde

Serves 4

Prep time
15 minutes

Cook time
25 minutes

You can use your favourite green leafy veg in this flavoursome Portuguese bean soup.

Ingredients
2 teaspoons extra-virgin olive oil
1 large onion, diced
4 bacon medallions, chopped
2 garlic cloves, crushed
½ teaspoon smoked paprika
1.2 litres chicken stock made using 2 cubes (ensure gluten free)
400g potatoes, scrubbed and roughly chopped
400g tin haricot or flageolet beans, drained and rinsed
150g Savoy cabbage, kale or spring greens, shredded

1 Heat 1 teaspoon of the olive oil in a large saucepan. Add the onion and fry for 5 minutes, or until softened. Add the bacon, garlic and paprika and a splash of the stock. Cook, stirring, for 2 minutes.

2 Add the remaining stock and the potatoes. Cover, bring to the boil, then reduce to a simmer for 15 minutes or until the potatoes are tender.

3 Add the beans and cabbage, kale or spring greens. Simmer, uncovered, for 2 minutes, or until everything is heated through.

4 Serve drizzled with the remaining oil.

SmartPoints values per serving 6
SmartPoints values per recipe 22

Cook's tip

Instead of beef, you could make this curry using turkey or chicken breast for 3 SmartPoints per serving.

MEAT

Beef rogan josh

A great dish for a weekend batch cooking session – serve half and freeze the rest for another day.

Serves 4

Prep time
25 minutes

Cook time
1 hour 15 minutes

Ingredients

Calorie controlled cooking spray
500g cubed lean braising steak
1 large onion, sliced thinly
2 carrots, sliced
3 garlic cloves, chopped
2.5cm-piece fresh ginger, grated
3 cardamom pods, split
1 teaspoon cumin seeds
1 tablespoon medium curry powder (ensure gluten free)
2 teaspoons paprika
1 teaspoon mild chilli powder
2 tablespoons tomato purée
300ml vegetable stock made with ½ cube (ensure gluten free)

1 Heat a large, heavy based, lidded pan over a medium heat. Mist with the cooking spray and cook the beef for 6 minutes until browned all over. Remove the beef and any juices from the pan, then set aside.

2 Add the onion and carrots to the pan and mist with more cooking spray, stir and cover. Cook the onion and carrots for 5 minutes over a medium heat until softened. Stir occasionally. Add the garlic, ginger, cardamom, cumin seeds, curry powder, paprika, chilli powder and tomato purée and stir to coat the vegetables in the spices.

3 Return the beef, and any juices, to the pan with the stock and bring to the boil, then reduce the heat to low and part-cover. Simmer gently, stirring occasionally, for 1 hour or until the beef is tender. Season to taste before serving.

SmartPoints values per serving 5
SmartPoints values per recipe 19

Pork vindaloo

Serves 2

Prep time
15 minutes
Cook time
10 minutes

Traditionally a hot curry, the yogurt will help to cool down the heat. If you prefer it spicy, leave it out!

Ingredients

Calorie controlled
cooking spray
250g lean pork loin steak,
cut into thin strips
1 onion, sliced thinly
1 red pepper, deseeded
and sliced
3 garlic cloves, chopped
2.5cm-piece fresh ginger,
thinly sliced
1 teaspoon cumin seeds
1 teaspoon ground coriander
½ teaspoon turmeric
2 teaspoons tomato purée
2 teaspoons cider vinegar
½ vegetable stock cube
(ensure gluten free),
crumbled
½ teaspoon dried chilli
1 tablespoon chopped
fresh coriander
2 tablespoons low-fat
natural yogurt

1 Heat a wok or large nonstick frying pan over a high heat. Mist with the cooking spray, add the pork, and cook for 2 minutes until starting to brown. Turn the pork and cook for another 2 minutes until cooked through. Transfer the pork and any liquid in the wok to a plate and set aside.

2 Reduce the heat slightly under the wok or pan and spray with more cooking spray. Add the onion and stir-fry for 1 minute, then add the red pepper, garlic and ginger and stir-fry for a further minute.

3 Add the cumin seeds, ground coriander, turmeric, tomato purée, vinegar, stock cube and dried chilli, then return the pork to the wok. Stir-fry for another minute and season with black pepper. Sprinkle with the fresh coriander and serve with 1 tablespoon of yogurt per person.

SmartPoints values per serving 6
SmartPoints values per recipe 12

Serves 4

Prep time
20 minutes

Cook time
35 minutes

MEAT

Chorizo & chickpea stew

There are lots of big, bold and satisfying flavours to enjoy in this authentic Spanish stew.

Ingredients

Calorie controlled cooking spray
1 onion, finely chopped
2 carrots, diced
2 peppers, deseeded and diced
3 garlic cloves, grated
1 red chilli, deseeded and finely chopped
75g chorizo, diced
1 teaspoon smoked paprika, plus extra to serve
¼ teaspoon cinnamon
1 tablespoon cider vinegar
400g tin chopped tomatoes
400ml chicken stock made with 1 cube (ensure gluten free)
400g tin chickpeas in water, drained and rinsed
200g bag spinach, washed
4 tablespoons reduced-fat soured cream
Handful fresh basil, torn

1 Mist a frying pan with cooking spray, add the onion and cook for 5-10 minutes or until softened. Add the carrots and peppers, and cook for 5 minutes. If it starts to stick, add a little water. Season to taste.

2 Stir in the garlic, chilli and chorizo and cook for 2 minutes, then add the paprika and cinnamon. Stir together and add the vinegar, tomatoes and stock. Bring to the boil, turn down to a simmer and cook for 10 minutes.

3 Stir in the chickpeas along with the spinach, and warm through until the spinach wilts. Serve in bowls topped with a dollop of soured cream, a sprinkling of paprika and basil leaves.

GF · 6 SmartPoints value

SmartPoints values per serving 6
SmartPoints values per recipe 22

MEAT

One-pan fry-up

Serves 2

Prep time
10 minutes
Cook time
20 minutes

Up the veg content in this easy weekend brunch dish by adding spinach or onions to the pan.

Ingredients
Calorie controlled
cooking spray
250g potatoes, cut into
2cm cubes
3 bacon medallions,
chopped
150g chestnut or button
mushrooms, sliced thickly
2 eggs

1 Spray a large lidded nonstick frying pan lightly with the cooking spray. Stir-fry the potatoes for 3-4 minutes over a high heat until starting to brown at the edges. Season, add 3 tablespoons of water and cover the pan. Cook, covered, for 5 minutes over a low heat, stirring once or twice, until the potatoes are almost cooked through.

2 Remove the lid, add the bacon and increase the heat to medium. Cook for 2 minutes, then add the mushrooms and cook for a further 2-3 minutes.

3 Make 2 spaces in the potato mixture and break an egg into each gap. Cover the pan again and cook gently for 2 minutes or until the eggs are cooked to your liking. Divide between warmed plates to serve.

SmartPoints values per serving 6
SmartPoints values per recipe 11

MEAT

Greek leftovers soup

Make Sunday's roast go further by using what's left in this hearty herby soup.

Serves 6

Prep time
20 minutes
Cook time
1 hour 25 minutes

Ingredients
**Calorie controlled
cooking spray
3 carrots, roughly chopped
1 onion, quartered
1 garlic bulb, sliced in half
(no need to peel)
2 litres hot vegetable stock
made with 2 cubes
300g leftover roast
lamb on the bone
2 bay leaves
120g pearl barley, rinsed
200g spring greens, chopped
2 medium eggs
Juice of ½ lemon
Small handful each of fresh
dill, fresh parsley and fresh
mint leaves, chopped, plus
extra for garnish
1 tablespoon extra-virgin
olive oil**

1 Mist a large heavy-based pan with cooking spray and put over a medium heat. Add the chopped carrots, onion and halved garlic. Cook for 5 minutes, stirring frequently, until the onion and garlic start to colour.

2 Add the stock to the pan along with the lamb, still on the bone, and bay leaves. Bring to the boil, then reduce the heat. Cover and leave to simmer for 45 minutes.

3 Strain, reserving the lamb, garlic and stock, discarding the rest. Add the stock only back to the pot.

4 Add the pearl barley to the pan and simmer for 25 minutes. Remove a ladleful of the stock, then add the greens and simmer for a further 5 minutes. Meanwhile, squeeze the garlic pulp into a small bowl. Add the eggs and lemon juice, and whisk until foamy. Stir in the reserved ladleful of stock.

5 Add the egg mixture to the soup and stir, seasoning well. Slice the lamb from the bone into the soup, sprinkle in the herbs and divide between bowls. Garnish with more herbs then drizzle over the olive oil and serve.

SmartPoints values per serving 7
SmartPoints values per recipe 43